God's Pencil

Poems by Debbie Baker

Copyright 2021
ALL RIGHTS RESERVED

No part of this work may be reproduced or transmitted by any means, whether electronic or mechanical, including photocopying and recording, or by any information storage or retrieval system without the proper written permissions of the copyright owner.

1. Religion 2. Poetry

ISBN: 978-0-578-91976-8

First Edition

Some of these poems previously appeared in a chapbook entitled *Hands to Thee*.

✝

Table of Contents

Forward i
Bread of Life 1
Consequences 2
Spirit and the Flesh 3
The Bible Truth 4
Priorities 5
Spiritual Side 6
The Covenant 7
Gain the World, Lose Your Soul 8
Jesus and a Man Named Simon 9
Greener Pastures 10
Body and Soul 11
Idle Time 12
Who Am I? 13
The Cornerstone 14
The Voice 15
Light with a Purpose 16
My Candle 17
Gifted 18
Believe 19
A City Called Heaven 20
All That I Am 21
Choices 22
Chosen 23
Different Day Same Story 24
Have a Big Heart 25
Heavenly Being 26
I'm Just Saying 27
Labor of Love 28
Life 29

✝

Palm Sunday 30
Prophet 31
Reason 32
Reflection 33
The Gospel 34
Vessel 35
Working in the Light of the Lord 36
About the Author 37

Forward

Having a passion for Christ fuels my desire for writing, with the hope that I may comfort, motivate, and encourage others to seek a relationship with Jesus Christ, because without him we are nothing.

Mother Teresa said it best, "I am nothing. He is all. I do nothing of my own. He does it. That is what I am God's pencil. A tiny bit of pencil with which he writes what he likes. God writes through us, and however imperfect instruments we may be, He writes beautifully."

Bread of Life

The bread of life is found in this Book
For this meal does not require a cook
On Sunday we receive the main course meal
Taken in by the Word, and all that you feel
Take time out to read the Bible each day
Daily nourishment for the mind, never losing your way
Hunger for the Word, always wanting more
For as filling as the Word is, it moves me to the core
So during hard times when you can't find your way
The question is, are you hungry, have you read your
  Bible today?

Consequences

Modern day religion has taken up the value of man
They have shortened the use of God's word to insert their own plan
Short-changers and thieves—around the altar is where they stand
Where they take from the House of the Lord straight out of God's hand
We come to the Lord's House for peace and to hear a word from God on high
But today's church is so filled with confusion God's message passes you by
I keep searching and searching but the church's help I cannot find
Any resolutions to ease or comfort my mind
You say God sees all inside
The true heart of a person, from God you cannot hide
So to all those in sheep's clothing, false prophets just you beware
If you continue these foolish games hell is not a dare

Spirit and the Flesh

Man in his present state is conniving and deceitful
Once made in God's image but now a mixture of good and evil
In him lie emotions of anger, envy, and jealousy which can be dangerous coming from the heart
But in the spirit there is only one emotion and that is love that sets them apart
Earthly desires and that of the flesh is one in the same
Being in the spirit one fights the desires of the flesh and there is no shame
Fleshly desires, deeds of our sins
It's only through the Holy Spirit that a person truly wins
Death only comes to those with a hardened heart, cold and heavy
But peace, joy, and love come to those who stay in the spirit, always praying, always ready
Remember from the time of Adam and Eve works of the flesh have been our stumbling block
So why not choose life now and walk by the spirit and let the Lord be your rock?

The Bible Truth

So you think the Bible is not true
It's filled with stories from prophets whom God had spoken to
Just as we have a last will and testament so is the Bible God's will
Told to the prophets for God's people to fulfill
Prophets empowered with miracles and deeds not of their own
With signs and wonders only God could have known
By the grace of God, scriptures are given with everything we need
Instructions through poems and parables with rules for spiritual life to proceed
Within these pages lie our belief in heaven, in Christ, and in our salvation
The Father, the Son, and the Holy Spirit the maker of all creation
Evidence which is written within these pages
Is proof that He is who he said He is down through the ages
To see is to believe, some would say
But blessed are the faithful, steadfast in that which is unseen and continue to pray
So you see, the Bible is not made up of what you can touch but what the heart can feel
And if God has touched your heart there is no doubt you know the Bible is real

Priorities

Should I or should I not? Most often times you will
Be so selfish as to go against His commandments and steal
Selfishly we never give them any thought before what we do or say
Not putting God first is the reason the world is in the shape you see today
First we must remove ourselves and put God in our plans
Because without Him there is no you, it's all like sinking sand
To Him I came broken and torn
A new life He gave me, now I am reborn
Renewed in the spirit, facing toward the light
A new creature walking by faith and not by sight
You see God is the reason I boldly speak out today
To spread the gospel of Jesus Christ because He is the way

†

Spiritual Side

All around us is the supernatural, yet a world away
Is another time like night is to day
Beyond this world is a spiritual place
Where good and evil battle face to face
Wages of war beyond what the eyes can see
Is the true battle between good and evil powers that be
Here the true nature of evil cannot hide
From the Guardian Angel that stands by your side
Rolling shadows, demons of the night
Guardian angels, protector of souls constantly fight
Those blinded by evil are unable to comprehend
That separation from God is hell in the end
Remember hearts filled with evil are incapable to feel
That the fight between angels and demons for our souls
   is real

The Covenant

For many years we've looked to the hills for help
With guidance from God we search for His footsteps
Like Moses on the mountain where all noise has ceased
On the mountain he found silence, a place of peace
High in the sky is a voice carried by birds
Listen to the mountains for a soft spoken word
Just as Moses, I, on my knees honor His Holy place
Thanking God for his many blessings with hands of grace
With Moses's safe return in his arms are instructions imprinted in stone, God's will
And it is by this covenant, through faith and obedience we are healed

Gain the World, Lose Your Soul

What does it profit a man to gain the world but lose his soul?
Would it be wealth, riches, diamonds, or gold?
Fancy clothes or an expensive car
To live in Hollywood to be a star
Material things fade away and rust
Disappearing as fast as the wind blows away dust
They know not the answer of true wealth
The way of this world only leads to death
To never have been told the love of Jesus is sad to say
Eyes blinded by Satan can't even find their way
True wealth money cannot buy
Like the love of Jesus and mansions in the sky
So what does it profit a man to gain the world but lose his soul?
Only a world of ungodliness drowning in sin
Until their hearts are open allowing Jesus to step in

†

Jesus and a Man Named Simon

Carrying the cross of Jesus was Simon's role in God's plan
Simon with his two children became curious and noticed on the street the bleeding, condemned man
Jesus of Nazareth beaten and filled with exhaustion
Simon of Cyrene, forced to carry His cross, approaches with caution
Simon's eyes encountered Jesus's eyes; he could not move or walk away
Moving closer to Jesus he listened and this is what Jesus had to say
"Come to me, you who are weary and burdened, and I will give you rest"
Simon, with fear in his heart, confessed
With just a touch from Jesus disappeared all his fear and fright
Jesus whispered, "I am gentle and humble in heart, for my yoke is easy and my burden is light"
As Simon brought Jesus and the cross near
Simon whispered, "If you need me Jesus, I am here"
With the stripes of pain Jesus still showed us love
Thinking of us, keeping with the Father, God above
So it is at Easter we pay remembrance to Jesus's death and celebrate the glory of His resurrection
For it is through Jesus Christ that our lives are given direction

Greener Pastures

A photo of deception is what the devil tries to hide
With illusions of the grass being greener on the other side
Pleasures of the eye lustful of the mind and flesh is the devil's path
Sinful we are by nature children of wrath
Things are not always as they seem we find ourselves not ready
Read and study God's Word so that you remain steady
No matter the situation be content in the here and now
Through faith listen and the Lord will show you how
Greener is the side
Where on the cross Jesus died
And rose with all the power in his hand
So don't be fooled, the side is greener where you stand

†

Body and Soul

There is this being that lives and dies
This physical body, by water we baptize
Washing away the old, and in with the new
By Jesus Christ made Holy are you
Your body does not define who you are as it grows and matures
But defined by the soul, both loving and pure
Have no fear of that which kills the flesh and not the soul
Our spirit in search of eternal life is the goal
Unsaved, we are born of the flesh
But reborn in Christ we are new and fresh
Remember the path to heaven is to accept the Lord's gift of salvation
And through Jesus Christ is the only way to God's heavenly creation

Idle Time

Being the product of idle time
Doing when and whatever comes to mind
Good and bad choices knowing the right things to do
Frightening, when it's the bad things we choose to go through
Free will, the choices that we make
The determining factor to which path our lives will take
Foundation, with rules from God plan
Good counseling, feet firmly planted in knowing where we stand
The sum of a decision today, is its consequences for tomorrow
Whether being a lifetime of happiness or a lifetime of sorrow
There is good and evil, right and wrong, and two sides to every story
But only right and just decisions reap rewards within God's Glory

Who Am I?

I am the brown clay God scooped from the sand
He molded me, then blessed me with His own hand
He breathed life into my lungs and sat me on the land
I am God's finest creation and he called me "man"
From clay to man He loved me all the while
"Who am I?" you may ask, I'm God's own child
In the blink of an eye he placed at my feet
A companion and all the food I could eat
So now I know. Just who am I?
God created and molded me from up on high

The Cornerstone

Building without knowledge they build by hand
All that they build has been done on sinking sand
But you must have a chief cornerstone where all others come together
A living stone that surpasses the test of time forever
All levels of stones, having different shapes firmly constructed into a solid foundation
The chief cornerstone is Jesus Christ, God's plan for our salvation
We need to build our lives on the strong foundation of Jesus and his Word
As servants of God, His message through others will be heard
Every person's gifts are built as one—what a great combination
Joined together into a Holy Temple of the Lord is Revelation
Whereby as this temple is consecrated, God lives by his spirit in us
Laid as the foundation, I Am, the cornerstone chosen and precious

The Voice

Developing a relationship with the one who transcends all
Just as a child learns to walk, he must first learn to crawl
The sound of thunder, wind, and rain means more than you think
They are echoes and the whispers of God's voice all in sync
The voice of God with each passing day amplifies
It is that relationship that allows us to recognize
That with every passing day an understanding of his voice becomes clearer
With the sound of his voice I am drawn nearer
So meditate and listen for what he has to say
And ask for understanding as you kneel before God and pray

Light with a Purpose

Where there is darkness, light will divide
There in the dark nothing truly hides
Sent from heaven among us the Son of God did stand
The Lamb of God with compassion for us, held out his hand
Light of the world straight from above
This light teaches us the importance of true love
It's the guiding force that shows us the way
This light with a purpose, it's to God we pray

Saul, who once persecuted Christians, was unknowingly surrounded by a glorious light
He saw and heard Jesus before losing his sight
While in a glorious presence a conversion took place in Saul
Due to this conversion his name was changed to Paul
Through the darkness this light will always shine
A ray of light that leads to the Great Divine
So remember that into each life some light must shine
Its guidance is mysterious, but yet adaptable is this light with a purpose for all to find

†

My Candle

The sparkle that flickers through the night
Eyes of the Lord with his flock in sight
I am the light, in darkness have no fear
Hands of guidance will keep you near
Keep your mind on God even in the darkest of hours
Having faith and strength in the Holiest of powers
Remember God gives all that you need, never lose sight
Warriors for the Lord, for Jesus Christ we fight

Gifted

Let those with voices loudly sing
With sounds rejoicing to the King
Giving lectures, a person gifted with speech
Will spread the gospel to all as they teach
Hands that draw freely upon any line
Hands that glorify The Great Divine
Being a true believer is one of the rules
Diligently, in harmony laboring with God's tools
Diversity of gifts given to each their own
Glorifying the King high upon His throne
Remember as one body all gifts work together
Spreading the good word of our Lord forever

Believe

The heavens and earth—their very presence came to be by a spoken word from God
What will it take for you to believe?
To receive and lose sight with just one command, to change a killer of Christians to a chosen vessel for the Lord
What will it take for you to believe?
Radiant in power with a touch of the hem of His garment it heals, He calms the raging seas and walks on water
What will it take for you to believe?
Beaten and battered not for what he's done but for what we've done, He lived a sinless life. No greater Love is there than one who will lay down his life for them
What will it take for you to believe?
God gave us his only begotten son that we may have eternal life, all He asks is that you believe.
Now tell me, what will it take for you to just believe?

A City Called Heaven

Heaven's a place we long to see
Now that Jesus has set us free
Where no one has hate or evil in their heart
Where we and our loved ones will never part
With streets of gold and a pearly gate
In God's hands lies our fate
A multitude of tribes from everywhere
Their faith in Jesus brings them there
God has prepared our mansions in the sky
Where there's no mourning, no pain, not a tear from
  our eyes
The presence of God forever in our midst
With a foundation of precious stones you can't resist
And we will sing Holy, Holy, Holy with the angels
What a magnificent thing
With eternity, forever, to praise the King

All that I Am

Through my pen, Lord, I ask that you bleed over this page so that they see your works and not me
When I first began to write it was my way of understanding God's word in terms that I could see
He took my love for writing and my love for Him and placed them hand in hand
To spread the love of Jesus Christ and to give an encouraging word to others, now I understand
That what He gives to me is not to be kept, but to be shared
Tried and true I learn to put my faith in you, no longer am I scared
But to be bold in knowing that I Am is with me
That this love of writing, this journey with Christ, He will see me through
So until the ink runs out and there are no more curves to be made, all that I am, your humble servant, I will always be
Your willing vessel Lord continue to use me

†

Choices

Every day carries its load of good and bad
God gives us free will to choose and a lot of times the choice we make is sad
We are so used to the wrong things that life has made our hearts numb
Things of this world made us forget where we come from
They do not see the day-to-day struggle
If you can never see that then you can never see the trouble
Our enemy stands by our side and plays the scripture game
Because he too was once an angel and he knows the scripture the same
So if you don't know, a fool you may be
All because you choose not to open your eyes to see
The one who came to set you free

Chosen

Chosen as His mouthpiece we are used
To help all those who are lost and confused
Chosen we are as His hands we labor
Through faith, hope, and love we care for our neighbor
Chosen we are through His eyes we are a witness
With powerful testimony to God's grace and goodness
Chosen we are as His feet we travel here and there
Spreading to all who will listen the gospel everywhere
One faith, one body, one spirit...The Holy Trinity life
　forever

Three that bear witness on earth Spirit, Water, and
　Blood.

1 John 5:8

Different Day Same Story

Even though each day is new the same story is being told
How the life of Jesus Christ through the Bible unfolds
The hard times and struggles they had back then
People still have today; it all boils down to sin
When Jesus spoke and performed miracles believers were set free
Today when He speaks or works a miracle we believe half of what we hear and none of what we see
From the beginning by God's spoken word everything came into creation
Man became overwhelmed by his own infatuation
Jesus was talked about and mocked over the things that he had done
We still fail to realize that it's only through Him that our battles are won
We battled then and now, constantly we fight
Let us not forget, with the dawn of a day a sunset will follow
And without the Lord, we're just a shell, empty and hollow

Have a Big Heart

How big is your heart?
When someone bumps you in a crowd are you easy to forgive them or do tempers flare in the moment?
How big is your heart?
When someone calls out your name do you turn and walk away, or do you turn to fight?
How big is your heart?
When you are driving and someone cuts you off do you say a few choice words, or do you let them have their way?
How big is your heart?
Christ was spit on, beaten, and yet he continued to have a big heart.
We have all at some point found ourselves in a situation with a small heart that never thought about the heart of others.
I encourage you the next time things do not go just as planned, know that behind the scenes, God's handling things. Not on our time but on God's time.
So, let it go and have the heart of Christ.

Heavenly Being

Heavenly angelic beings flying above the throne of Grace
The closeness of God, too powerful to behold with wings they cover their face
Because their feet are considered unclean
They too are covered not worthy to be seen
Around the Throne, beside it, are angels that praise God on high
Holy, Holy, Holy is the Lord Almighty the eternal song they sing to God constantly to glorify
God's Holy domain they guard, they protect from sin
Known as the Throne Angels they allow no corruption to enter in
Gabriel special messenger in the presence of God he stands
Delivering instructions from heaven to earth as God commands
Guardian Angels we are given to show us the way
Unaware of their presence they protect and guide us each day
So as Multitudes of Heaven, God's bidding is what they do
With messages from heaven straight to me and you

I'm Just Saying

Why fight, to all He gave life
The same air we all breathe
When cut we all bleed
We all have the same right
To breathe in, to breathe out
To live and to die
I'm just saying

How can we as people expect to
Bring about a change
One bullet, no name, lives lost
It's all the same
We all have the same choices in life
Will it be heaven or hell?
I'm just saying

Wake up people, that's what it all
Boils down to
This life is a gift, the present treat it as such
As you are blessed be a blessing to others
I'm just saying

Labor of Love

I may not have a degree, my words are not that advanced
Who am I to be given any chance?
Nor do I lavishly dress
As the Lord flows through my mind on paper I express
The Lord has a way of getting His work done
It is a labor of love working for the Lord, God's son
The choices He makes are not for me to understand
Being called for his purpose, God's plan
It does not matter the clothes or the education of a man that He chooses
But the heart and soul of a person that He uses
Jesus's disciples, each different from the other, yet hand picked
To do the work of the Lord they were perfect
So, no matter the character of a person the Lord makes a way
Trust and believe, seek him daily, and most of all pray

Life

It is by the fruit of the spirit where in joy, love, and peace you live
It is looking toward the skies day and night knowing that God of all is in all
It is when you close your eyes and your mind meets comfort and peace
It is at that very moment that the body begins to feel all negativity release

It's the in and out of every breath that you take
It's but a whisper that vanishes with the change of the wind
It's the day of awakening from a long night's slumber
It's the rain and lightning with a clash of thunder

It's miraculously from out of the clay formed man and from his rib came forth a woman
Pondering things such as these of life in so many ways
So you see it is but when your soul thirsts only the living water of Christ can fill
Life, it's that presence of joy and peace that no other has the power to steal

Palm Sunday

Every year they celebrate the Holy week
Sacrificing the best of the best for the fest
One year they heard that Jesus was joining the celebration
The Pharisees wanted to know the man that had caused them frustration
As Jesus entered Jerusalem, palm branches they would lay
Humbly he came on a donkey colt, with cloaks and palm branches paving the way
The closer Jesus came, the bigger the crowd grew
All wanting to see the prophet, the miracle worker they knew
Humbly on the back of a donkey in would ride Israel's King
"Save us, King of David, Hosanna to the highest," they would sing
What Jesus instructed his disciples; they did not understand the task at hand
But later at the resurrection it became clear their part in His plan
That Jesus of Nazareth is "The Lamb of God" that is the reason he came in
Because to the world He became the sacrifice to take away our sin

Prophet

Godly talents are given to some to understand the insides peek
Some people have dreams awake as well as asleep
With encouragement we bow our heads and pray
Directions, warnings to help others along the way
As a part of this body we all have a job to do, it's the Lord's will
In His footsteps on this path of faith it's God I feel
Godly children with eyes and ears open know the deal
That Satan only comes to rob, kill, and steal
Remember all the talents in this one body of Jesus Christ is strong
With God's protection you'll never go wrong
So to all the dreamers—stay focused and on track
Helping those, through the darkness, find their way back

Reason

Mary, by the Holy Spirit conceived
The Son of God in whom He is well pleased
We celebrate for this reason
Our Lord and Savior is all about this season
This is the meaning of why we are here
To honor the Lord Jesus Christ, the blood sacrifice we hold dear
Because of the love He has for you and I
Nailed to a wooden cross they hung Him to die
On the third day He rose with all power in His hand
Given dominion over the heaven and the earth is God's plan
Skeptical they were about the resurrection, yes it's true
That He died for me and He died for you
Told to the prophets in scripture of His return
It took eye-witness testimonies for them to learn
That what is for God, death has no grip, our Redeemer lives
And it's eternal life to all He gives
Life, freely He gave up his own
Now seated by God, at His right hand upon the throne

Reflection

Mirror, mirror through you I examine me
Taking close inventory of the person I turn out to be
How often do I give thanks before I eat?
Am I always nice to all those I meet?
Am I always kind and polite in what I say?
And just how often do I take out the time to pray?
A daily struggle from the flesh within
An everyday task to fight against sin
I see a life filled with confusion
But by God's grace He has shown me Satan's illusion
He wanted to look like, and sound like God, Satan knows how to be a twin
That's why he was cast from heaven because of his sin
Mirror, mirror to thine own self be true
Because when you lie to me, you lie to you
As I look into my eyes, Lord let your light shine
A light that only you can give, the light of the Great Divine
Satan has fed you lies through the mirror on the shelf
So now take inventory, have a real talk with Jesus and open your eyes to His vision of yourself

The Gospel

The gospel, stories of emotion, making you smile and cry
Followers of Jesus, they testify
To the life and time of Jesus, to His death on the cross
Ye of little faith all was not lost
Death on the cross, by His blood we are saved
"But how?" they ask, when He rose from the grave
Matthew and Mark tell of the miraculous events that surround His virgin birth
And as an exorcist, healer, and miracle worker while he was here on earth
Luke speaks of Jesus being the Son of God, haven't you heard?
How John testified to His resurrection, just look to the Bible to study His word
So they testified of the life of Jesus, a man whose life was without sin
Written for us the New Testament, is the Gospel of four men—Matthew, Mark, Luke, and John.

Vessel

Molded and shaped upon the wheel
The potter uses his special skill
The finest of things made to hold
A unique vessel more precious than gold
Just as He commanded the light to shine
This vessel, too, is one of God's great designs
Tarnished it can become by this thing called sin
Which causes hatred and destroys the soul within
Made of clay it carries a precious treasure
Beyond anything that you or I can measure
The treasure of life and all that it contains
Are in this vessel with its cracks, chips, and stains
Just as He positioned heavenly bodies in the sky, like a star
In the image of God, this vessel, know that is who you are
This vessel molded and shaped like the heavens above
And made precious in His sight because of His love

†

Working in the Light of the Lord

The pressures of life may sometimes weigh you down
Stolen joy can turn a smile into a frown
Dread and despair will only keep you sinking
Lighten your load with positive thinking
Set apart some time from each day
To say a prayer and let the Lord lead the way
Stepping stones, a set of trials, know that is what life is
In this life imitate Christ make your heart like His
Because the answers we seek are not given by man
Jesus is the answer, and God has the plan

†

About the Author

Debbie Thomas Baker was born and raised in the small town of Reeltown, Alabama. As an adult, she rededicated her life and became a member of Hicks Chapel Church where Rev. Pearl Clark was the pastor at the time. And it is through the passion that she has for the Lord that she writes.

Her father Wesley Thomas and her mother Floria Watson have passed on. She has two amazing children Sir Thomas (son) and Tequilla Thomas (daughter) and one beautiful granddaughter, Payton Stalling.

Baker has one previously published book of poetry entitled *Inspirational Poems with Power* which is available on Amazon. She can be reached for readings by contacting her directly by email or phone:

ordebbiebaker095@gmail.com

(334) 415-3553

www.ingramcontent.com/pod-product-compliance
Lightning Source LLC
Chambersburg PA
CBHW072022290426
44109CB00018B/2316

SHE: I never did no such thing.

HE: Double negative, double negative.

SHE (*Washing dishes*): You can be so aggravating. God!

HE: There you did it again.

SHE: You don't give me a moment's peace.

HE: But that's all I want from you. (*He pats her fanny.*)

SHE (*Slapping him with the dishcloth*): Stop that, you dirty old man.

HE: I am *your* dirty old man. Your very own, very dirty old man. Come here. You want to clean me? Come on and clean me good. (*He hugs her and she responds, laughing.*)

(*In their clinch they change to a faulty plug in a wall socket.*)

SHE: What's wrong? I feel you've slipped.

HE: It's my left prong. The screw hole's stripped, I think.

SHE: Your lamp's blinking.

HE: I know. I know. The whole thing will blow out if that jerk don't put down his newspaper and screw it back in.

SHE: Not him again. He's so inept.

HE: She's better.

SHE: She can hold a wratchet at least.

HE: Can you give me more juice?

SHE: Don't be unintelligent.

HE: Can't you do something?

SHE: I can be constant, that's something.

> (HE *starts to shake her.* HE'S *pulling her out of a car. It's raining and they're on a curve of the highway at night.*)

HE: You stupid woman driver, do you know what you've done to my car? You shouldn't be driving. What are you—drunk or something? The curse? What excuse can you give me, can you give God? Do you know what's under that crushed door in the suicide seat of my car? We were taking a ride in the rain. My mother likes rain. I'm going to make you see her. I'm going to make you look at her. By the time I get through with you, you'll be behind bars for the next ninety years. (HE *opens her car door, still holding on to one of her shoulders, and drags the terrified woman from behind the wheel.* SHE'S *numb and in a state of shock.*)

SHE: It's raining. It's dark. It's raining.

HE: It's raining. It's beautiful. Why didn't you open your eyes? Do you have a license? I bet you don't have a license. How could you be allowed to drive? I wasn't going more than thirty-five. (*He pulls her close.*) Ahhhhrg, you've been drinking! Disgusting. It's too much.

SHE: It's my birthday. It's raining.

HE (*Propelling woman toward his car, he forces her head down to look at mangled body of his mother*): There! That's what you've done, you—you—you miserable!

SHE: Oh my God! Oh my God! She's still holding on to her purse. She's holding on to her purse like a little girl. She's still holding on.

HE (*Pulling her around*): I'm going to make you know what it feels like to have your face crushed in. (*He forces her down onto the road and is about to jump on her head.*)

(HE *becomes a pencil writing a list.* SHE *is the list and says the list as* HE *writes it with his body.*)

SHE: Take car to be greased.
Pick up shirts.
Check on George.
Go to Joe's workshop.
Plan the next five years.
Get new underpants.
Mail letters on way home.
Stop at Roger's to get the key.
Check on Mozart Masses.
Attend Mr. Jordan's funeral.
Take car to be greased. (HE *topples over to land beside her.*)

(*In bed in early morning*)

SHE: Honey?

HE: Arhgghhhh.

SHE: Alarm.

HE: Grrrrrrr.

SHE: Get up.

HE: Uhhhhhhhhhhhh.

SHE: Get up.

HE: Ghhhhhhh.

SHE: Get up.

HE: Fuck it.

SHE: Not now.

HE: Arghhhhh.

SHE: Honey?

HE: O.K.

SHE: Honey?

HE: O.K.

SHE: Alarm.

HE: O.K.

SHE: Get up.

HE: O.K.

SHE: Honey?

HE: O.K. . . . (HE *leaps straight up in the air.*)

    (*A living room.* HE *paces,* SHE *sits.*)

HE: I don't know why you expect so much. What more do you want? What else can I do? I'm here. I'm here with you. What else can I do that I'm not doing? What is it? I can't make it out. You don't tell me, yet—you want. You want. I can feel you crouched there inside that mound of you. And I know you want. But I don't know what it is that you want. What is it? Do you want it? Do you? You don't know what it is I'm talking about, do you? You don't—do you? And yet you sit there and you want. You want, you want. And I stand here, and I don't know what it is that you want, you want. I stand here, don't I? At least I'm here. I'm here with you. Look? See? Your man is here. Right here, see? Two arms, two legs, only one head, just like everybody else. Yet, you want. I feel that tug in you. Where do you want me? What do you want of me? Backward and forward, you want!

(SHE *cries.*)

HE: That's what you wanted? That's what you wanted? That's all you wanted. Cry? That's too easy. You can't get out of it that way. It's another trick to get me off the track. I'm going to find out if it takes me the rest of my life. I'm going to find out what it is you want. Do you hear me? I'm going to find out if it takes me the rest of my life. . . . The rest of my life! (SHE *begins to smile a tiny smile to herself.*)

(SHE *rises to face him. Their bodies and faces take on Kabuki-like attitudes. The banal lines should be intoned with whining but amplified sounds as if calling to the dead.*)

HE: Where are you going?

SHE: To wee-wee.

HE: Good girl. When will you be back?

SHE: When I finish.

HE: Good girl. Bring me a cigarette.

SHE: In a minute.

(*They change exact positions.*)

SHE: Where are you going?

HE: Bowling with the boys.

SHE: Good boy. When will you be back?

HE: When I finish.

SHE: Good boy. Bring me a cigarette.

HE: In a minute.

(*Repeat above scenes three times. Then they relax into postures of American Indians in a cave.*)

HE: Morning Star?

(SHE *smiles weakly.*)

HE: Mine.

SHE: Hot.

HE: Morning Star. (*Caresses her face.*)

SHE: Cold.

HE: Morning Star. (*Strokes her hair.*)

SHE: Hot.

HE: Food?

>(SHE *shakes her head.*)

HE: Love?

>(SHE *nods.*)

HE: Morning Star. (HE *sits near her and puts his blanket around them both.*)

SHE: Hot.

HE: Mine.

>(*A diner—* HE *orders breakfast. Matter-of-fact.* SHE'S *the waitress, casual.*)

HE: Orange juice.

SHE: Yes.

HE: Squeeze yourself?

SHE: Yes.

HE: Two fried eggs.

SHE: Yes.

HE: Sunnyside up.

SHE: Yes.

HE: Bacon.

SHE: Yes.

HE: Three pieces.

SHE: Yes.

HE: Not too well done.

SHE: Yes.

HE: Toast.

SHE: Yes.

HE: Two pieces.

SHE: Yes.

HE: Buttered.

SHE: Yes.

HE: Hash browns.

SHE: Yes.

HE: With onion.

SHE: Yes.

HE: Coffee.

SHE: Yes.

HE: Dark.

SHE: Yes.

HE: Water.

SHE: No.

> (*Breakfast at the diner. Master—slave. Waitress is master.*)

SHE: Orange juice.

HE: Yes.

SHE: Squeezed.

HE: Yes.

SHE: Two fried eggs.

HE: Yes.

SHE: Sunnyside up.

HE: Yes.

SHE: Bacon.

HE: Yes.

SHE: Three pieces.

HE: Yes.

SHE: Not too well done.

HE: Yes.

SHE: Toast.

HE: Yes.

SHE: Two pieces.

HE: Yes.

SHE: Buttered.

HE: Yes.

SHE: Hash browns.

HE: Yes.

SHE: With onion.

HE: Yes.

SHE: Coffee.

HE: Yes.

SHE: Dark.

HE: Yes.

SHE: Water.

HE: No.

> (*Breakfast at the diner. Master—slave. Customer is master.*)

HE: Orange juice.

SHE: Yes.

HE: Squeeze yourself?

SHE: Yes.

HE: Two fried eggs.

SHE: Yes.

HE: Sunnyside up.

SHE: Yes.

HE: Bacon.

SHE: Yes.

HE: Three pieces.

SHE: Yes.

HE: Not too well done.

SHE: Yes.

HE: Toast.

SHE: Yes.

HE: Two pieces.

SHE: Yes.

HE: Buttered.

SHE: Yes.

HE: Hash browns.

SHE: Yes.

HE: With onion.

SHE: Yes.

HE: Coffee.

SHE: Yes.

HE: Dark.

SHE: Yes.

HE: Water.

SHE: No.

(Breakfast at the diner—Automation. Both behave like pre-programmed robots. Square gestures, equal space beween words, and perfectly equal time between question and response.)

SHE: Orange juice.

HE: Yes. Squeeze yourself?

SHE: Yes. Two fried eggs.

HE: Yes.

SHE: Sunnyside up.

HE: Yes. Bacon.

SHE: Yes. Three pieces.

HE: Yes. Not too well done.

SHE: Yes. Toast.

HE: Yes. Two pieces.

SHE: Yes. Buttered.

HE: Yes. Hash browns.

SHE: Yes. With onion.

HE: Yes. Coffee.

SHE: Yes. Dark.

HE: Yes. Water.

SHE: No.

> (*Breakfast at the diner—Bliss. Customer and waitress have symbiotic ecstatic relationship. Played with quiet warmth and secure joy.*)

HE: Orange juice.

SHE: Yes.

HE: Squeeze yourself?

SHE: Yes.
HE: Two fried eggs.
SHE: Yes.
HE: Sunnyside up.
SHE: Yes.
HE: Bacon.
SHE: Yes.
HE: Three pieces.
SHE: Yes.
HE: Not too well done.
SHE: Yes.
HE: Toast.
SHE: Yes.
HE: Two pieces.
SHE: Yes.
HE: Buttered.
SHE: Yes.
HE: Hash browns.
SHE: Yes.
HE: With onion.
SHE: Yes.
HE: Coffee.

SHE: Yes.

HE: Dark.

SHE: Yes.

HE: Water.

SHE: No.

          (HE *leans on her as they struggle forward.*)

HE: We've walked miles.

SHE: Only a bit more.

HE: Give me some water.

SHE: We're out.

HE: I can't move.

SHE: Yes. Only a little way yet.

HE: Leave me here.

SHE: No.

HE: My stomach aches.

SHE: It'll stop.

HE: Farther?

SHE: Only a bit.

HE: Can you see?

SHE: Yes.

HE: How much?

SHE: Enough. There, just there, a little beyond.

HE: Thirsty.

SHE: Me too.

HE: Kiss?

SHE: One. (*A brief kiss.*)

HE: How much farther?

SHE: Only a bit. (*They fall asleep standing in place.*)

(*Waking up, still standing in place.*)

SHE: Honey . . .

HE: Mmmmmmmmmmm.

SHE: Love you . . .

HE: Good girl . . .

SHE: Really love you . . .

HE: My doll . . .

SHE: Honey?

HE: I'm here.

SHE: I hate you to leave me.

HE: Is it the alarm?

SHE: Sorry, darling.

HE: Not your fault.

SHE: Angel, hold me one more time.

HE: One more time.

SHE: One more time.

HE: One more time.

SHE: Till tomorrow morning.

HE: Till tonight.

SHE: Lover?

HE: Tonight.

SHE: Tonight?

HE: You better believe it.

SHE: Bye bye, baby . . .

HE: Honey?

SHE: Now.

> (*They assume a Kabuki posture and* SHE *starts to move away from him.*)

HE: (*Kabuki voice*): Where are you going?

SHE: (*Kabuki voice*): To wash the clothes.

HE: Good girl. When will you be back?

SHE: When I finish.

HE: Good girl. Bring me a cigarette.

SHE: In a minute.

> (*They walk toward each other and collide. They pick each other up, threaten with arms and feet, then turn and walk away.*)

SHE: Where are you going?

HE: Crazy, wanna come along?

SHE: Good boy. When will you be back?

HE: When I finish.

SHE: Good boy. Bring me a cigarette.

HE: In a minute.

> (*They change exact physical places and stances with one another, asking each other casually, "Where are you going? Where are you going?" Then they intone: "Crazy wanna come along? Crazy, wanna come along?"*)
>
> (*A kitchen.*)

SHE (*Her back to him*): I know you're here.

> (HE *smiles.*)

SHE: I know you're here.

> (HE *approaches.*)

SHE: My back's shivering.

> (HE *smiles.*)

SHE: I feel lighter. I know you're here.

HE: I've been gone a long time.

SHE: It doesn't matter.

HE: You've waited?

SHE: What else?

> (*He smiles.*)

SHE: You're here. All of you. You're here.

HE (*Embracing her*): We're here.

SHE: Let me turn away again.

HE: Why?

SHE: I want you all around me.

HE: Like this? (*Encircles her from behind.*)

SHE: Oh yes. Yes. Yes. Just like this. Yes.

> (HE *picks her up and holds her aloft.* HE *puts her down and smiles.* SHE *picks him up, holds him aloft, then drops him.* HE *falls and stays on the floor.*)

HE (*The rich man, Luke 16: 19. In hell in torment*): Father Abraham, have mercy upon me. Send Lazarus to dip the tip of his finger in water to cool my tongue; for I am tormented in this flame.

SHE (*as God*): Son, remember that you in your lifetime received your purple and fine linen and fared sumptuously every day: and Lazarus a beggar was laid at your gate full of sores. He asked only to be fed with the crumbs which fell from your table; moreover, you fed him not, but moreover, your dogs came and licked his sores, but now he is comforted here (*heaven*), and thou art tormented. And besides all this and moreover, between us and you a great chasm has been fixed, in order, moreover, that those who would pass from here to you may not be able to, and none may cross from there to us.

HE: I pray thee therefore, father, that thou wouldst send him to my father's house. For I have five brethren; so that he may testify unto them, lest they also come into this place of torment.

SHE: They have Moses and the prophets; let them hear them.

HE: Nay, father Abraham; but if some one went unto them from the dead they will repent.

SHE: If they hear not Moses and the prophets, neither will they be persuaded even though some one has risen from the dead.

(They rise and raise their hands above their heads. They study their hands. They lower their hands and look at them. They fit their hands one into the other. They look at each other. They pull their hands apart and the man and woman lace their hands together. They look down at their interwoven hands. They look into each other's eyes. Still with hands locked, HE *leads her to a chair and seats her. Then their hands break apart.* HE *pats her shoulder.)*

(We are now in a police station.)

HE: There now. Pull yourself together. It isn't as bad as all that. Stop crying, for God's sake. I'll just phone your husband, and we'll try to get this straightened out.

SHE (*Alarmed at word husband*): No, don't call him. Wait, yes, do call him. I did it for him.

HE: You mean your husband put you up to pulling the robbery?

SHE: It's his fault. It's all his fault. The lazy buzzard.

HE: You mean he wouldn't do it himself?

SHE: Wouldn't do nothing for himself. I still have to cut his veal steak for him. After forty years of marriage, he still hasn't learned to cut the meat on his own plate. I cut it into tiny cubes, "bite size," he says. But still he don't say thank you. No, not once. Not one thank you in forty years of marriage.

HE (*Filling out report form*): Now, how much money did you get?

SHE: Almost two hundred.

HE: I have to know the exact amount.

SHE: A hundred eighty-five dollars. I got that from the Jay Hacock Mutual Life.

HE (*Fast and angry—a technique*): Were you also the hooded bandit who robbed the Murcury Loan Company of five hundred dollars on February twenty-eighth at four-thirty P.M.?

SHE: Don't shout at me.

HE: Sorry, ma'am. Just doing my job. This robbery you pulled was a lot like the one at Murcury.

SHE: What's murcury?

HE: I want you to identify the items I'm going to show

you. The matron removed them from you when we brought you in.

SHE: Where's my gun?

HE: I can't let you have it.

SHE (*Pitifully*): It isn't a real gun.

HE: It's evidence and belongs to the state.

SHE: What ever am I going to tell Stanley?

HE: Stanley?

SHE: My grandson, Stanley. He belongs to the track team, and that's the gun they use to start the races. He'll never forgive me.

HE: Please, ma'am, if you'll just pull yourself together and identify these things, I'll let you call Stanley to explain.

SHE: I'll try.

HE: Have you ever seen this black hood before?

SHE: Of course, I put it on in the washroom, before I went and robbed the insurance company. That's where I left my white hat.

HE: If you hadn't left that hat, we'd never have found you.

SHE: I don't care. Just wait till he gets home from work.

HE: Is this jacket . . . ?

SHE: Who'll cut up his meat in tiny cubes tonight, huh? Who do you think will do it?

HE: Is this jacket yours? Are these black slacks yours?

SHE: Yes. I bought them at our church rummage sale so you couldn't trace the labels.

HE: Where's the money?

SHE: What money?

HE: The hundred eighty-five you got away with.

SHE: Oh, that?

HE: Did you hide it in your home?

SHE: Now, that would be pretty dumb!

HE (*Intimately*): If we get the money back, the judge will go easy on you.

SHE: I don't want special treatment. Tell them to lock me up and swallow the key.

HE (*Fast and angry*): Where's the dough?

SHE: I won't tell.

HE: Please, lady, what'd you do with it?

SHE: I gave it away.

HE: You risked grand larceny to give the money away?

SHE: I put ten dollars in the hand of every bum on Third Avenue.

HE: The shit you did! Er, excuse me, ma'am.

SHE: Mister. When my husband comes to the station house, do you think, would you mind—I mean I'd like to borrow your handcuffs to wear for our interview. I know he'll carry on and try to hug me. But I want to be wearing those handcuffs so I won't have to hug him back.

(*A night club.*)

HE (*A comedian at a mike*): So these fuzz busted me and dragged me to the local jug. And the judge lays the rap on me, see. And he says to me I'm obscene, see. He says to me I'm obscene, that I talk dirty. That I talk sexy and arouse the aroused, that I don't know what I'm talking about, see, but if I didn't know what I'm talking about, how could I arouse all those dead dongs, see? And like the whole time I'm fishing my pocket for my pocket mirror and I gets it out and flash it at him, see. And I yells this is my sex detector Tester, see. And like he's nearsighted and I shove it right into his chops and I says, "If you're confused about sex," I says, I shove this here mirror right up to his whiskers, and the nose hairs of his nostrils tickle the top of the glass. And I says to him I says, "If you're confused about sex, yer honor, then hold this down to your crotch (unzipped, of course), and see if it'll mist up the glass. And if it don't, call in the firemen, cause you need a shot of novocaine in yer balls." And then he says to me . . .

SHE (*Drunk*): Go on home, yer mother's calling your mouth for soapysuds, dirty little boy.

HE: And then he says to me . . .

SHE: Out! With soap. Whyn't someone wash that loud mouth out with soap. He don't drink. He's too young.

HE: Will someone lay that broad in the mouth so that I can continue my dissertation?

SHE (*Jumping up with glass*): I'll do it myself. You mother!

HE (*Keeping mike between him and woman*): You get pimples that way, lady.

SHE (*Trying to hit him*): Stand still so I can put a stop to you.

HE: Husband? Husband of this drunk. Get up here. Your wife is making an ass of you.

SHE: Come here, you dirty rotten two-bit little East-side snot-snarf. I can teach you a lesson, if I could just reach you.

HE: Back to your table, cow pie.

SHE: Greaseball.

HE: You're so sloppy you have to home permanent your snatch.

SHE: Bastard, bastard.

HE: Beast, beast.

SHE: Bugger.

HE: Bug.

(*They become galaxies sending radio signals to each other.*)

marvelous chance comedy that resulted from one personality taking over a role begun by a quite different personality—sometimes in mid-sentence.

We staged the play in the center of the café, with a small bench for the men on one side and another for the women on the opposite side. The person who spun and called sat in full view of the audience and behaved with the attitude of an official at a tennis match or basketball game. The women were dressed in tights and simple free-flowing colorful dresses. The men wore white ducks and brilliant hockey jerseys. There were three small white boxes and one white platform for them to work with. The platform at times doubled as a throne, a sailing ship, and an Indian pony. The resourcefulness of the players seemed boundless and grew with every performance.

Besides being great fun to watch and do, the play can train the actor in concentration, focus, flexibility, and ensemble work. The words are there and in a firm enough situation so that the main equipment of the actor is free to fly once the technical part of the play is under his belt. I like to think of the play as a trampoline for actors and director. We played with three men and three women. But more or fewer would work. It could even be done as a straight transformation play with one man and one woman. The director should feel free to cut any scene he and the actors can't solve.

PRODUCTION NOTES

∎

This play is meant for both actors and audience to be an enjoyment of technique—pure virtuosity on the part of the actors. The fun of the play is in how much and how involved the audience gets. When we did it at Café La Mama Experimental Theatre Club, some people came three nights in a row to see it. It was never the same play. I've thought since that we should have done it twice in one night. The play taxes not only the actor's imagination, but his physical prowess, team ability, and intellect.

It can be approached in two ways, and I know an imaginative director will find others. We played it with a small card on which all the actors' names were printed. A wheel was spun by a disinterested party at intervals of thirty-five to ninety seconds. A name was called out and one actor ran into the play and another actor ran out.

I had originally thought the director would sit on one of the benches with the actors and send them in as a coach does at a basketball game, and I'd still like to try this. However, it might take away from some of the

SHE: Bleep Bleep. (*She moves in steady orbit.*)

HE (*Moving in a faster, more irregular orbit, sometimes slow, sometimes like a dervish, always in opposition to her rhythm*): Blink blink blink.

SHE: Bleep blink bleep blink bleep blink blink.

HE: Blink, blink, bleep bleep blink bleep bleep blink.

SHE: Bleep bleep blink blink bleep.

HE: Blink blink blink blink bleep blink blink bleep.

SHE: Bleep bleep bleep bleep blink bleep bleep blink.

HE (*Slowing*): Blink bleep blink.

SHE: Bleep blink bleep.

HE: Bleep bleep.

SHE: Blink blink.

HE: Bleep.

SHE: BLINK.

(*They come abreast and salute. They are members of a cub scout troup.*)

TOGETHER: "... and to the republic for which it stands, one nation indivisible, with liberty and justice for all." (*They put their hands like goggles over their eyes and sing*):

Up in the air, Junior Birdmen,
Up in the air upside down,
Up in the air, Junior Birdmen,
With your shoulders to the ground.

(*Chanting*):
It takes five wrappers,
Four box tops,
Three pop sticks,
Two bonbons,
One thin dime.

(*Singing*):
Up in the air, Junior Birdmen,
Up in the air upside down,
Up in the air, Junior Birdmen,
With your shoulders to the ground.

(SHE *looks far away, as if out to sea.* SHE *gestures to him to look too.* HE *comes close to her, and very slowly they sink to the floor and* SHE *pulls him on her lap and holds him as if he is a small boy.*)

SHE: Once upon a time when we lived on the beach we were hungry. You dug us a clam. You put the clam shell on a rock studded with white barnacles. We hid in a tide pool and waited for the sea gull to dive, feet first, at the clam. ZZZZZzzzzzzzzzzzeeeeeeeeeeeeeeeeeeee, down came the gull and got the fat clam then dropped it from above and split the fat clam in two. We ran screaming to the rock and fought the sea gull for the fat juicy clam. And then we sat in the sand and ate and ate and ate and ate till the clam juice ran into our bellybuttons. That was the best clam we ever had.

HE: The best.

SHE: The absolute best.

> (HE *pulls away from her, still crouching. They both pull blankets around them Indian style. They're huddling under a lean-to. It's cold.*)

SHE: Red feather.

HE: Mmmmmmmmm.

SHE: Red feather.

HE: What?

SHE: Why are you silent?

HE: What is there to say?

SHE: Red feather?

HE: Yes.

SHE: Say it.

HE: Say what?

SHE: You want to go away from me.

HE: Maybe.

SHE: So go.

HE: In a while.

SHE: Then I'll go.

HE: All right.

SHE: Keep well.

HE: You too.

SHE: The sun is out.

HE: At last.

    (SHE *is arriving home after a long absence.*)

SHE: Dad?

HE: Who . . . is it . . . Sharon?

SHE: Yes.

HE: Sharon.

SHE: Yes.

HE: It's been a long time.

SHE: It doesn't seem like it now.

HE (*Looking at her face, pointing out some tiny lines*): You didn't have this one, or this one, or that one.

SHE: I know.

    (HE *pulls away.*)

SHE: Dad?

HE: Didn't get much fishing done. Water was too high this year, swept away all the eggs. Fish had a hell of a time trying to spawn too.

SHE: You sound the same.

HE: You don't.

SHE: How's the family?

HE: Same as ever.

SHE: You seem younger. I mean, *you* haven't changed.

HE: I guess not.

SHE: What is it?

HE: Eyes watering, that's all.

SHE: Can we take the boat out?

HE: Why, sure. Why, sure we can.

SHE: Let's go.

HE: Now?

SHE: Why not? It's been a long time.

HE: The tide's right.

SHE: Let's go.

HE: Like old times.

SHE: Like old times.

(*A bedroom.* SHE *is packing and* HE *unpacks her things as* SHE *packs them.*)

HE: You're not leaving this house.

SHE: I can't help it.

HE: What do you mean you can't help it?

SHE: I can't. I can't help it.

HE: Of course you can help it. You can stay.

SHE: No.

HE: Don't say that. You can't say no to me. Not after all we've been through together. You can't walk out on me. We've survived everything, everything. You can't take that away. You can't leave.

SHE: I've got to.

HE: I forbid it. I forbid you to leave my bed.

SHE: That's why.

HE: That's why what? That's why what?

SHE: You're smothering me.

HE: You! I'm smothering you! Me! What about me? I'm the one who's been smothered around here, but I survived. I survived.

SHE: I can't help it. I'm sorry, but I can't stay.

HE: You're going to stay.

SHE: I can't. I can't help it.

HE: You're going to help it. You're going to face it. You're staying here.

SHE: I'm not.

HE: You are.

SHE: You disgust me.

HE: Big news.

SHE: You disgust me!

HE: And you know what you do to me?

SHE: I'm getting out.

HE: Not without me, you're not.

> (HE *picks her up and carries her to a rock near the ocean.* HE *wants her to give him a feeling of permanence. Repeat this scene three times.*)

HE: Have you known me long?

SHE: Yes.

HE: How long?

SHE: Long.

HE: How long?

SHE: Your eyes have green flecks at the center.

HE: How long?

SHE: Your nose has a small dimple here.

HE: Will you know me long?

SHE: Yes.

HE: How long?

SHE: Long.

HE: How long?

SHE: You have tufts of fur on your shoulder blades.

HE: You can never leave me.

SHE: I won't.

HE: How can I be sure?

SHE: You can be sure.

HE: How?

SHE: The bones of your feet remind me of dinosaurs.

HE: You do know me.

SHE: Yes.

HE: You do!

SHE: I do.

HE: You have known me.

SHE: Yes, it has been long.

HE (*Comforted*): You know me.

SHE: I know you.

> (*Jubilant,* HE *takes her hand and they leap to their feet and run with a leaping step to an open grassy field. This is based on a polka, a dance of joyous courtship.*)

HE: Inside.

SHE: Outside.

HE: All around.

SHE: Up and down.

HE: Turning.

SHE: Gliding.

HE: Inside.

SHE: Outside.

HE: Right along.

SHE: Galloping.

HE: Jump.

SHE: Catch me.

HE: Sweet.

SHE: Hard.

HE: Hold on.

SHE: Tight.

HE: Upsadaisy.

SHE: Inside.

HE: Outside.

SHE: Shall we go in?

HE: Right away.

SHE: Inside?

HE: IN!

>(*All the actors join together for the final scene. This should be carefully staged and played warmly to the audience. It is to be sung and gracefully danced.*)

HE: Haven't I met you somewhere before?
    On the steps of Elsinore?

> At the film of Eleanor?
> Just inside the Barbary Shore?

SHE: No, no no, I don't think so,
> Although I'd like to slip with you behind the door.

HE: What more, what more, what more
> Could any man ask of a new maid?

SHE: Then shall we slip,
> Then shall we dip,
> Into a love time,
> Travel to a hot clime?

HE: What more, what more, what more
> Could any man ask of a new maid?

TOGETHER:
> Then we'll dip,
> We'll slip,
> We'll glide,
> We'll hide.
> We'll slide
> Into love time,
> Into love time,
> Into love time.
>
> Then we'll dip,
> We'll slip,
> We'll glide,
> We'll hide.
> We'll slide

Into love time,
Into love time,
Into love time.

Love time,
Love time,
Love time,
Love time,

INTO LOVE TIME!

    CURTAIN

Also By
Megan Terry

Approaching Simone

Calm Down Mother

Comings and Goings

Do You See What I'm Saying?

Ex Miss Copper Queen On A Set Of Pills

The Gloaming, Oh My Darling

Hothouse

Keep Tightly Closed In A Cool Dry Place

Megan Terry's Home Or Future Soap

The People Vs. Ranchman

The Tommy Allen Show

Viet Rock

Please visit our website **samuelfrench.com** for complete descriptions and licensing information

OTHER TITLES AVAILABLE FROM SAMUEL FRENCH

APPROACHING SIMONE
Megan Terry

Bio-Drama / 8m, 4f, plus ensemble

Simone Weil, a French girl of Jewish extraction whose death in 1943 was caused primarily by self-imposed starvation, is the subject of this striking theatrical exploration into the nature of faith and spirituality. *Approaching Simone* gives fascinating insights into this extraordinary woman who was later canonized as a saint.

Winner! Obie Award as Best Play of 1969-70

"A superb theatrical coup."
– *The New York Times*

"May very well stimulate renewed interest, especially among the young, in one of the most powerful minds and tormented spirits our age has produced."
– *Newsweek*

SAMUELFRENCH.COM

OTHER TITLES AVAILABLE FROM SAMUEL FRENCH

THE PEOPLE VS RANCHMAN
and
EX-MISS COPPER QUEEN ON A SET OF PILLS
Megan Terry

15 or more m & f / Platform set
The People vs Ranchman - Ranchman is brought to trial for raping two women, a girl and a boy. With some calling for his death and some for his liberation, he is electrocuted. He reappears from the grave and is confronted again by his accusers. The victims reenact the rapes and this time Ranchman is both hung and shot. In the third segment, Ranchman in eternity is again confronted by his accusers. This time they beg forgiveness, dramatically demonstrating that we are all both guilty and innocent for the evil in the world and therefore cannot kill a man for sins willed to him.

3 f / Exterior
Ex-Miss Copper Queen on a Set of Pills - A former beauty contest winner, disowned by her family after the birth of her illegitimate child, is sleeping off wine and goofballs in a skid row doorway. Two refined female winos who collect things from garbage cans they can hock come along. The "Queen" parts with her bottle for a peek at the "baby" in the carriage. She believes she sees her child, slumps and passes into eternity.

SAMUELFRENCH.COM

OTHER TITLES AVAILABLE FROM SAMUEL FRENCH

THE GLOAMING, OH MY DARLING
Megan Terry

4m, 6f / Interior

Two old crones in a sanitarium fill their day with fantasies. The dead husband of one is nearby and the other proclaims her marriage to him. After visits by vapid children with grandchildren, after the bland services of the nurse and further sexual fantasies, the two decide to share the husband. This is enough to raise him from the dead and induce him to reminisce about the wild West. At last night comes.

SAMUELFRENCH.COM

www.ingramcontent.com/pod-product-compliance
Lightning Source LLC
Chambersburg PA
CBHW072022290426
44109CB00018B/2315